ANGEL MOON
DIARY

2020

Angel Moon Diary 2020

Copyright © 2019 by Mystic Cat

www.mystic-cat.com

Acknowledgment:

I would like to express my gratitude to my family,

who support and nurture my dreams.

Time is set to Coordinated Universal Time Zone (UT±0)

The Archangels

Archangels are always around you, sometimes you need one particular angel, more than another. Depending on your current life circumstances, one or more angels will be walking the journey carefully with you. Archangels come into our lives with their love, understanding, and compassion. They work for the highest spirit and seek to protect and empower you to be the best version of yourself. They encourage and support us. Archangels come to us with love, acceptance, understanding, and deep compassion. You can call on your archangels whenever you need guidance and support, they send you love and blessings, and bring the knowledge that you never walk alone. Here are the 15 main known Archangels and their role in your life.

Archangel Ariel ~ Lioness of God

Ariel is the guardian and healer of animals. Call upon her when you seek to communicate with animals that have passed over or are in your life. Ariel also rules over the natural world, and when in nature, she is nearby. She is warm and hospitable with a caring, sensitive environment. Her energy is powerful yet gentle. She inspires natural growth and encourages people to live to their full potential. Her role is to make you aware of the vital role that animals can have in your life, as they do provide a close network of support, which is essential to nurture the gifts of empathy and compassion. Animals are a blessing in our lives, and should always be treated with love and compassion. Kindness to all animals in general associates with healthful benefits that draw abundance into your life.

Archangel Azrael ~ Whom God helps

Azrael is often described as the Angel of Death. Do not be scared of this title as, like the tarot card, he offers you transformation during difficult times. He provides comfort for families and friends who are grieving the loss of a loved one. For those who have crossed over, he guides them to the light to reconnect with their loved ones in the spirit world. He offers compassion and wisdom. His energy is comforting, patient, and understanding. His words are softly spoken, He says that your loved ones are a gift from heaven which return to source when their earthly work is done. Always appreciate the moments you are blessed to spend with them, the very knowledge that these gifts are borrowed from heaven, and can be recalled at any time enable you to appreciate the blessings they bring to your life. After losing a loved one, call on his support for healing.

Archangel Chamuel ~ He who sees God

Chamuel embodies generosity, love, and compassion. He makes us more aware of the love and compassion in ourselves, understanding the grace we hold within our spirit also allows us to attract more positivity into our environment. He is also known for helping to raise intuition and spiritual vibrations, and for helping us to tune into channeled messages from the divine and higher spirits. His energy is loving, tender, and sympathetic. He is warm and delightful, a good listener with a generous and open heart. Chamuel helps balance interpersonal bonds and draws the right people into your journey. You can also call upon him to protect your world and create barriers from the nefarious individuals who are not on a higher level of evolution and do not resonate genuine kindness and compassion to others. It is his work to help find the right people for your journey in this world. He offers protection from those who would do harm.

Archangel Gabriel ~ Strength of God

Gabriel heightens creativity, giving you the ability to develop your inherent gifts of writing, art, music, verbal expression, and emotional expression. .Gabriel is graceful, elegant, and uplifting. Her words are positive, encouraging, and inspiring. She communicates her wisdom with the intent of creating positive change and growth. You can call upon Gabriel when you need help understanding, accepting, and passing messages from the spiritual realm. Gabrielle offers strength, guidance, and acceptance. She resonates with the message of taking that which cannot be changed, but looking for solutions to create the shift you would like to see in the world. So much is within your grasp if you allow your vision to take flight. Your ideas have wings; they seek manifestation in your life.

Archangel Haniel ~ Grace of God

Haniel brings gifts of heightened intuition, receptivity, and self-awareness in divination. Haniel guides those who seek to develop their psychic abilities, spiritual talents, and even healing arts. Her energy is healing, soothing, and patient. She helps restore equilibrium and is a profoundly caring Angel. She offers relaxation with her gifts of uplifting your spirit and rejuvenates your soul. She is colorful, nurturing, and conscientious. She speaks with thoughtfulness and understanding, call on her for words of wisdom, grace, and knowledge. If you are interested in the esoteric arts, she is your go-to Angel if you want to increase your intuitive and psychic abilities.

Archangel Jeremiel ~ Mercy of God

Jeremiel is the Angel of faith and hope, he is one of the main Archangels who help people cross over to the spiritual realm. He guides souls to review their life on earth and helps people learn from their mistakes. He also brings prophetic dreams and visions. Jeremiel resonates with the energy of compassion and mercy. He enables you to gain insight into areas which feel murky, he illuminates a path forward, which helps dissipate the fog, and this allows you to gain clarity. Call on him. If you seek to understand a situation better, and his wisdom shines an intense beam forward, allowing you to discover the truth.

Archangel Jophiel ~ Beauty of God

Jophiel helps us when we feel lost. She lets us become aware of the grace and beauty in our souls, she doesn't focus on physical attractiveness. She teaches people to search deep within themselves and gain the confidence needed to express openly from the heart. She helps us see the beauty in others and in our environment, so we can appreciate and be grateful for what we have. Jophiel is gracious, inviting, and elegant, she speaks softly and in gentle tones. She reminds people who they really are inside and what they can become if they set the bar higher, for themselves, and for those around them.

Archangel Metatron ~ Highest of Angels (twin)

Angel Metatron is a twin of Sandalphon, they were both once human but ascended as Angels. He is connected to the Book of Life and takes meticulous records of all that happens on earth. He helps those who need motivation, discipline, and organization. He can help those who are starting a new endeavor or project and need help with time management or organization. His energy is connected to the essence of being human. Because he was once human, he understands essential human traits and weaknesses. Archangel Metatron offers down to earth advice, he is direct and analytical. He can assist you with practical matters.

Archangel Michael ~ One who is like God

Archangel Michael, one of the best-known Archangels and the Angel who was even featured in a blockbuster movie, he is called upon often by those who are currently eath bound, Michael is accommodating when it comes to spiritual protection and cleansings. He is everyone's favorite protector and guardian, Michael possesses strength and courage. Archangel, Michael helps connect you with your destiny and actual life purposes. He can clear out any negative energies which are around your life. Archangel Michael is a big personality who has an enormous presence in your life, his keen sense of purpose enables you to move out of your comfort zone, and release doubt, dispel fear, and move beyond your limitations to achieve your loftiest goals. He is ethical, righteous, and one who has firmly held ideals. He is selfless, disciplined, with a genuine desire to improve your life by releasing all barriers which keep your potential held back.

Archangel Raguel ~ The friend of God

Archangel Raguel is the Angel of Justice, Raguel resonates truth and honesty. He presides over our lives as a mediator, helping us in challenging situations. He restores balance and equilibrium; he draws peace and wellbeing into our environment, and he can also help resolve issues that cause stress or anxiety. His energy embodies logic and unbiasedness. Archangel Raguel is practical and offers realistic and achievable solutions. Justice is his passion, he is passionate and dedicated in his quest to correct the world's wrongs. He is righteous, an Angel who is tenacious with a sturdy inner shield.

Archangel Raphael ~ God heals

Raphael draws inner and outer healing (mental, emotional, physical, spiritual), this improves our lives by promoting better health and spirituality. Archangel Raphael is loving, kind, gentle, and compassionate. He is a genuinely caring person who was profoundly ethical. His big heart knows no boundaries. Raphael comforts and heals past and present emotional wounds. Raphael helps you to improve emotionally, mentally, even physically. Archangel Raphael helps release toxic energy, which drains your inner reserves. He is a magnetic and warmhearted Angel, whose purpose is to improve your emotional terrain. Raphael sees your life as a journey of self-discovery, Raphael wants to see you inspired, and ready to embark on new adventures. He wisely knows that creating a stable foundation is the first step in achieving your highest result.

Archangel Raziel ~ Secrets of God

Archangel Raziel heightens our faith and belief in the divine and the spiritual world. He possesses a profound understanding of life, he encourages us to strengthen our bonds to the spiritual realm and to seek help and guidance from the wisdom of the divine and the Archangels. Raziel is mature and wise. Raziel is direct, intelligent, and insightful. Raziel helps you to restore faith, trust, and confidence. Having a strong sense of belief in the divine is positively associated with longevity, it supports your well-being in a myriad of ways. Raziel is pleased to be there to support your personal growth.

Archangel Sandalphon ~ Highest of Angels (twin)

A twin of Metatron, and one of the two twins who were once human, but have since ascended into being Angels. He is connected to the Tree of Life. He makes us aware of our connection to both earth and heaven. Sandalphon was once human, he understands your weaknesses and fragility. He is the energy link between man and spirit, so his energy is swift and powerful. He is a messenger, bringing news from the divine. This will connect with your destiny correctly and with precision.

Archangel Uriel ~ The light of God

Archangel Uriel seeks to empower and enlighten you. He is a channel for higher wisdom and learning. Call on Archangel Uriel when you need to elevate your soul and spirituality. Archangel Uriel owl is an eccentric; he has a love for innovation and creative solutions. He feels that perception is everything, thinking outside the box, does light a path towards the realisation of your goals. This angel is self-sufficient, practical, and rational. He is generally interested in being of service in your world. He has a sense of humor and leaves curious signs which capture your interest, to guide your path forward.

Archangel Zadkiel ~ The righteousness of God

Zadkiel helps us with forgiveness and healing. He reminds us of the past and present, helping us to understand and accept milestones in our life journey. He gives us the strength to confront our wounds, and he also reminds us to be grateful and appreciates the gifts which surround our daily lives. His energy is gentle, subtle, and inspirational. His words are always calm and sympathetic. He teaches us to be accepting of others, to gain an understanding of different perspectives, and to forgive. Zadkiel helps you with emotional healing and forgiveness or to remove emotional blocks, whether it forgives yourself or about forgiving someone else.

January

Mon 30

Tues 31

Wed 1

New Year's Day

Thurs 2

January

Fri 3
First Quarter Moon in Aries. 4.45 UTC
Quadrantids Meteor Shower. Jan 1st-5th. Peaks night of Jan 3rd.

Sat 4

Sun 5

Message
Overall, your conditions are changing, this leads to more personal growth, and a desire to expand your life. Your restless spirit is sending vibrations out to the universe, this is connecting you with a flow of abundance, new options are coming, which will support a journey of change. A new destination is coming, life picks up the pace, it is an active and dynamic time ahead. You are ready to release the holding pattern, which has kept you stuck. This paves the way for a substantial chapter that allows opportunities to come through that perfectly align with your gifts.

January

Mon 6

Tues 7

Wed 8

Thurs 9

January

Fri 10

Full Moon in Cancer. Wolf Moon. 19:21 UTC
Penumbral Lunar Eclipse.

Sat 11

Sun 12

Message

Your intuition is activated when the secret information is revealed. This is by no means of full disclosure, a few juicy tidbits of gossip cross your path. It does see some emotional words come gushing out unfiltered, this gives you insight into an area which had felt like an ending, now things come full circle, this touches you down on a chapter which offers to bring changes to your life and sees more self-expressive energy flowing across.

January

Mon 13

Tues 14

Wed 15

Thurs 16

January

Fri 17
Last Quarter Moon in Libra. 12.58 UTC

Sat 18

Sun 19

Message
Your Angel says to expect wonderful epiphanies soon. He says that this is a time which is ripe with new projects and dreams; it does leave you feeling enthusiastic, your potential is on the rise, the news is coming, which helps you plan future goals. This is a time which offers you a fresh start, epic potential arrives to grow your talents. It does stoke the fire of your enthusiasm, this is a chapter which provides new pathways towards excellence. Change is in the air, it is shifting your focus forward, and this does provide further options. Evaluating your larger goals during this time is also highly beneficial.

January

Mon 20
Martin Luther King Day

Tues 21

Wed 22

Thurs 23

January

Fri 24
New Moon in Capricorn. 21:42 UTC

Sat 25
Chinese New Year (Rat)

Sun 26
Last Quarter Moon in Scorpio. 21.10 UTC

Message
Your Guardian Angel says to stay true to yourself when information is revealed soon, which may lead to changes to your friendships and interpersonal bonds. It does provide you with new information, and this may see your path diverging from your current social environment, in time it may draw an entirely different circle of friends, these are people who are on the same page, they understand your current mindset. You have a desire to shift camps and detach from the drama by choosing healthy bonds, this is the right path to evolve your life.

January

Mon 27

Tues 28

Weds 29

Thurs 30

January/February

Fri 31

Sat 1

Imbolc

Sun 2

First Quarter Moon in Taurus. 1.42 UTC.
Groundhog Day

Message

You have a guardian angel in heaven, she says that you have done an enormous job of advancing your life, she sees how hard you work, it does show you are on the right track, things are set to improve, as you see signs of things coming together, you can appreciate your refusal to give up and your willingness to persevere, even in the face of adversity. She says to look for sweet signs from heaven arriving for you soon, she sends her love.

February

Mon 3

Tues 4

Weds 5

Thurs 6

February

Fri 7

Sat 8

Sun 9

Full Moon in Leo, Supermoon. Snow Moon. 7:33 UTC

Message

Archangel Michael says some positive news is coming soon, this lights a path towards abundance. It does spark your interest and leaves you feeling motivated to draw something new into your life. He says you are highly creative, focusing on new projects is close to your heart. It is an ideal time to infuse your talents into a new venture, which inspires your mind.

February

Mon 10

Mercury at largest Eastern Elongation.

Tues 11

Weds 12

Thurs 13

February

Fri 14
Valentine's Day

Sat 15
Last Quarter Moon in Scorpio. 22.17 UTC

Sun 16

Message
Archangel Metatron, says that information is received and which cracks open the situation that had left you feeling confused. It is an ideal time, you start to think that you can make progress, it leaves you feeling strong and able to take on developing a situation which is close to your heart. Objective reasoning sees confusion and doubt being released. It does point a path towards clarity and insight once you have all the information at your disposal.

February

Mon 17
Presidents' Day

Tues 18
Mercury Retrograde begins

Weds 19

Thurs 20

February

Fri 21

Sat 22

Sun 23

New Moon in Aquarius. 15:32 UTC

Message

Archangel Sandalphon sends his blessings, he says, you can create the changes necessary to spark a revolution in your life. As you release stress and deal with the demands on your time, you clear a path that offers a superb outcome. Complexities that have held you back are no longer an issue. You are ready to light a route towards a new chapter of potential, it does blend your talents into a potent mix of manifestation.

February

Mon 24

Tues 25
Shrove Tuesday (Mardi Gras)

Weds 26
Ash Wednesday

Thurs 27

February/March

Fri 28

Sat 29

Sun 1

Message

Archangel Heniel showers you with angel dust, she says, maintaining balance will be a valuable tool as the pace becomes more active. Opportunities are arriving to explore; it takes you on a journey of learning and adventure. Getting out of your comfort zone, lets you explore these curiosities. There is magic brewing, it draws new options that alleviate boredom, and it gets you stepping out of your usual routine.

March

Mon 2
First Quarter Moon in Gemini. 19.57 UTC

Tues 3

Weds 4

Thurs 5

March

Fri 6

Sat 7

Sun 8

Message

Archangel Arial says you may feel restless, it is time which draws transformation into your life, and gives you new options to contemplate. As you awaken to the potential possible, you shift towards change and create a path that is in alignment with your real vision. It may find you walking some original parts, learning new areas, and liberating your life in ways that have you tuning into your true desires.

March

Mon 9

Full Moon in Virgo, Supermoon. Worm Moon. 17:48 UTC
Mercury Retrograde ends.
Purim (Begins at sundown)

Tues 10

Purim (Ends at sundown)

Weds 11

Thurs 12

March

Fri 13

Sat 14

Sun 15

Message

Archangel Jophiel says you sync up with an opportunity soon. It infuses your imagination with creative inspiration. You dive into an exciting chapter of exploring the local events and social invitations around your life. It draws lively conversations and deepens existing friendships. A close friend shares private information with you. It does bring clarity into your most important bonds. This person offers wisdom, enlisting the help of another draws support, it does bring new options to head out and about. You encounter someone who sparks your curiosity soon, this could even lead to a new friendship blossoming.

March

Mon 16
Last Quarter Moon in Sagittarius. 9.34 UTC

Tues 17
St Patrick's Day

Wed 18

Thurs 19

March

Fri 20

Ostara/Spring Equinox. 3:50 UTC

Sat 21

Sun 22

Message

Archangel Azrael sends you blessings. He says you enjoy both change and stability in your life, it does have you feeling at odds when you feel restless, and thirst for adventure, yet need to stay grounded. Having new options ignites a creative aspect of your life, it does see you transform your world, and awaken to the bounty which tempts you towards growth. You are ready for a new quest, information is looming to pave the way.

March

Mon 23

Tues 24

Mercury at most substantial Western Elongation.
Venus at most substantial Eastern Elongation.
New Moon in Aries. 9:28 UTC

Weds 25

Thurs 26

March

Fri 27

Sat 28

Sun 29

Message

You have gifts that nurture others, and it does lead to strong bonds being forged, which will carry you forward over time. You Angels say that life is becoming more social and may draw new friends into your life. It is a time of abundance and harmony, a project you get involved with takes flight. A theme of home and family is going to be prominent for you in the chapter ahead. It does elevate your situation and draws opportunities that offer you a wonderful sense of kinship and connection. It is a time with more responsibility, and this influences your life positively through the attainment of stability and structure.

March/April

Mon 30

Tues 31

Weds 1

First Quarter Moon in Cancer. 10.21 UTC
All Fools/April Fool's Day

Thurs 2

April

Fri 3

Sat 4

Sun 5
Palm Sunday

Message

Archangel Gabriel says that there is a reconnection looming, it does seem more open communication, helping to release outworn energy, and create space for a new chapter of potential to arrive. This is precisely when lovely things start to happen, it does put you in a perfect place to reignite this bond. It is a new season of potential, and it sees strength and perseverance coming out on top. A decision made cracks open an original path with this person. This is not a time for overthinking, tune into your dreams, be fully present as you explore an avenue which glitters with enticing options.

April

Mon 6

Tues 7

Weds 8

Full Moon in Libra, Supermoon. Pink Moon. 2:35 UTC
Passover (begins at sunset)

Thurs 9

April

Fri 10

Good Friday

Sat 11

Sun 12

Easter Sunday

Message

Archangel Jophiel says that your home and family is going to be a big focus, something is reaching a culmination, it does show the long-awaited goal is coming closer. It is a harmonious chapter that lights up potential in your home life. It does see things unfolding gently, the potential is ripening, a situation is set to blossom. A burst of new energy gives you wings and lets you plan for the future. It is an exciting time where you can upgrade your situation.

April

Mon 13

Tues 14
Last Quarter Moon in Capricorn. 22.56 UTC

Weds 15

Thurs 16
Passover ends

April

Fri 17

Orthodox Good Friday

Sat 18

Sun 19

Orthodox Easter

Message

Archangel Uriel says that it is a landmark time which sees remarkable growth occurring in your life. Events moved quickly forward, the pace is active but not chaotic, you structure adequately to maintain the demands on your time while keeping your energy balanced. There are those in your life who support your goals every step of the way, this offers you a valuable sense of support. Something is really to blossom in your life, opening a gateway forward.

April

Mon 20

Tues 21

Weds 22

Lyrids Meteor Shower. April 16th-25th. Peaks night of April 22nd.
Earth Day

Thurs 23

New Moon in Taurus. 2:26 UTC
Ramadan Begins

April

Fri 24

Sat 25

Sun 26

Message

You grow stronger through the trials you overcome, says a gentle Angel who visits you often. Archangel Zadkiel shares that you have spiritual gifts and a knack for tapping into your intuition. It does help you clarify and reveal information. When you feel a strange sensation in your gut, you can bank on the messages it sends you. Shifting your focus towards developing your talents will lead you on a journey that offers wisdom and growth. You are inherently creative, artistic, and expressive.

April

Mon 27

Tues 28

Weds 29

Thurs 30
First Quarter Moon in Leo. 20.38 UTC

May

Fri 1

Beltane/May Day

Sat 2

Sun 3

Message

The theme of this week represents harmony, Archangel Gabriel says that it's going to be busy ahead, remember to take time out of your schedule to nurture your soul and rebalance your energy. Structuring in self-care does enable you to heighten your productivity. Overall, it is a time that offers you room to stretch your talents and flex your abilities. It does set your potential on fire as a big project or deal makes itself known to you soon.

May

Mon 4

Tues 5

Weds 6

Eta Aquarids Meteor Shower. April 19th - May 28th. Peaks night of May 6th.

Thurs 7

Full Moon in Scorpio, Supermoon. Flower Moon. 10:45 UTC

May

Fri 8

Sat 9

Sun 10

Mother's Day

Message

You dial up a sense of potential this week as Archangel Jophiel says that if you've had issues with something being postponed, this is set to change as life becomes more active. A shift forwards takes you towards a more socially involved chapter; invitations are arriving, which spark your inspiration. A wide variety of options are likely to crop up and tempt you to get more engaged with life. This influences the drawing of harmony into your world for a good reason.

May

Mon 11

Tues 12

Weds 13

Thurs 14
Last Quarter Moon in Aquarius. 14.03 UTC

May

Fri 15

Sat 16

Sun 17

Message

You are working hard to improve your situation, and Archangel Zadkiel says that it is the time that draws new options into your life; this gives you a foundation you can grow. You can reap the benefits of expansion, staying open to new offers does heighten the potential possible. You are ready to evolve your situation and create the space necessary to bring something exciting into your life. It is a time which draws a refreshing option, it gives you an adventurous phase of going after your dreams.

May

Mon 18

Victoria Day (Canada)

Tues 19

Weds 20

Thurs 21

May

Fri 22

New Moon in Taurus. 17:39 UTC

Sat 23

Ramadan Ends

Sun 24

Message

There is plenty to look forward to ahead says Archangel Jophiel, she sees that you discover an area that relates to being of service, giving back to your wider community is something which feeds your passion. It does offer you a path that is in alignment with your higher values. There are encouraging signs coming which relate to developing your career, a pathway, you gravitate to positions you beautifully towards achieving your dreams. Adding a creative spark, lets you think outside of the box and discover a new option.

May

Mon 25

Memorial Day

Tues 26

Weds 27

Thurs 28

Shavuot (Begins at sunset)

May

Sat 30

First Quarter Moon in Virgo. 3.30 UTC
Shavuot (Ends at sunset)

Sun 31

Message

Archangel Ariel says that swinging out of your comfort zone draws new options. It could bring an exciting opportunity which broadens your horizons, learning, and knowledge are at the basis of this productive phase. You're hungry to create space to develop your situation, planting the seeds, does see something inspirational, crop up, which is a perfect fit. You're ready to harness a more proactive approach, something arrives which sets your life on fire with potential. Being mindful of your goals helps take down the barricrs, it lets you harness an air of manifestation, and sees you taking a dive into new territory.

June

Mon 1

Tues 2

Weds 3

Thurs 4

Mercury at Greatest Eastern Elongation.

June

Fri 5
Full Moon in Sagittarius. Strawberry Moon. 19:12 UTC
Penumbral Lunar Eclipse.

Sat 6

Sun 7

Message
You are ready to enter a new chapter of growth and development. Archangel Zadkiel says that if you feel stuck, unsettled, or unsure about which path to take, a decision made at this time is instrumental in paving the way forward. It relates to achieving the highest result possible and getting a better grasp on the road ahead. Strategy, planning, and creating the changes necessary are all going to be essential in allowing you to move forward. You can create dramatic change, listening to your intuition removes the clamor of distractions.

June

Mon 8

Tues 9

Weds 10

Jupiter at Opposition.

Thurs 11

June

Fri 12

Sat 13

Last Quarter Moon in Pisces. 6.24 UTC

Sun 14

Flag Day

Message

Archangel Uriel says that it is a time of releasing outworn energy, which has created turbulence in your life. Someone in your life has caused a disruption, releasing the past, does shift your focus towards a new chapter of potential. News arrives, which has a substantial impact on improving your situation; it lets you fully resolve to open your life to new options. Picking up the pieces after a problematic chapter is never secure, but does lead to fantastic new potential.

June

Mon 15

Tues 16

Weds 17

Mercury Retrograde begins.

Thurs 18

June

Fri 19

Sat 20

Sun 21

New Moon in Cancer. 6:41 UTC
Midsummer/Litha Solstice. 21:44 UTC
Annual Solar Eclipse.
Father's Day

Message

Archangel Chamuel sends blessings. He says someone of importance makes a daring debut in your life soon. It may have you wanting to rush into a situation, but taking time to build the foundations, does see you revealing long term emotional security is possible. This is someone who appreciates your thoughtfulness and feels compelled to get in touch often and nourish the bond. It is a friendship that offers room to grow into a relationship that supports your goals. It's a lovely friendship and companionship. It does slowly alchemize into your social and family life, helping to heal old patterns that limited progress.

June

Mon 22

Tues 23

Weds 24

Thurs 25

June

Fri 26

Sat 27

Sun 28

First Quarter Moon in Libra. 8.16 UTC

Message

Your fiery nature comes in handy as you commit to achieving your highest, says, Archangel Gabriel. She says, implanting yourself into a new environment is going to give you options that inspire. Look at projects in your wider community, there is a path which starts out small, but grows into a journey which offers many new experiences and friendships. She says that it's time to nurture your life and plant the seeds which grow into something special. It does see several associations emerging, leading to new projects, activities, and outings. Having a fresh makeover to your social circle does wonders.

June/July

Mon 29

Tues 30

Weds 1

Canada Day

Thurs 2

July

Fri 3

Independence Day (observed)

Sat 4

Independence Day

Sun 5

Full Moon in Capricorn. Buck Moon 4:44 UTC
Penumbral Lunar Eclipse.

Message

Archangel Ariel says that this is an ideal time to dig deep and explore your inner realm. This offers a fruitful opportunity for emotionally processing, and soul-searching. You must reflect and begin exploring the ideas which could take you on an expansive journey. Shed your outworn layers, and embrace a fresh chapter of potential. This is a great time to nurture your life. It does let you distance yourself from those who are disingenuous, if people are not stepping up and being transparent, shed the outworn skins, and circumstances that go along with areas that drain your precious energy.

July

Mon 6

Tues 7

Weds 8

Thurs 9

July

Fri 10

Sat 11

Sun 12

Last Quarter Moon in Aries. 23.29 UTC
Mercury Retrograde ends.

Message

Essential information is coming, which helps you manage your long-term goals. It brings a turning point and draws insight into the path ahead. There is merit in developing your talents, attaching your gifts to a way which grows your potential, is going to attract abundance. It brings tangible benefits that reflect the success of your abilities. You are going through a shift which may change your priorities, it sees you feeling inspired to expand your life. With something right around the corncr, you receive information which motivates. This leads to an active cycle, as you embrace planning your dreams.

July

Mon 13

Tues 14

Jupiter at Opposition.

Weds 15

Thurs 16

July

Fri 17

Sat 18

Sun 19

Message

Pinpointing a specific goal sees taking the correct action steps to make it happen. Archangel Metatron speaks of heightened creativity arriving, he says you are ready to improve stability, you set foot on solid ground when the area you contemplate does stir a new vision of potential. Your imagination runs wild, this draws new dreams and leads to an active cycle. You discover little to hold you back, you release the fear, and reveal a path which shimmers with new discoveries. It does seem your creativity is sparking with golden ideas.

July

Mon 20
New Moon in Cancer. 17:33 UTC
Saturn at Opposition.

Tues 21

Weds 22
Mercury at Greatest Western Elongation.

Thurs 23

July

Fri 24

Sat 25

Sun 26

Message

Archangel Jophiel says that you may feel restless, and that's okay. It does help to keep your options open, a path you take draws new friendships to light. It does offer you a chance to expand your life and embrace a new inspiration. It leaves you feeling refreshed and ready to take on the world with people who understand your mindset. She says information arrives soon, which is the catalyst for change. It does inspire the creative side of your mind and could see some significant improvements occurring. Surprises abound, things move in a positive direction. An influence of opportunity seeking to make itself known.

July

Mon 27

First Quarter Moon in Scorpio. 12.32 UTC

Tues 28

Delta Aquarids Meteor Shower. July 12th – Aug 23rd. Peaks night of July 28th.

Weds 29

Thurs 30

July/August

Fri 31

Sat 1

Lammas/Lughnasadh

Sun 2

Message

Metatron smiles warmly and says, you are ready to create space for something new. In fact, he feels you're doing the right thing by expanding your horizons. It helps you shut the door on a painful chapter. As you forge ahead, your priorities shift; you discover an area that shows promise. It is an essential process that draws new options to light and leads to change. There is an opportunity for growth on the horizon. Streamlining your schedule pays dividends. Not only does it heighten your productivity, but it also creates space to take advantage of an offer that arrives soon.

August

Mon 3

Full Moon in Aquarius. Sturgeon Moon. 15:59 UTC

Tue 4

Wed 5

Thurs 6

August

Fri 7

Sat 8

Sun 9

Message

Archangel Raguel says life holds a refreshing change, it's about expanding your world. It takes you to new places, experiences, and destinations. Currently, you may feel restless or unsettled. These vibrations arrive to shift your focus towards change. Your vision gains momentum, it brightens your life and inspires you to reach for more. It's an ideal opportunity to tackle your dreams; you enter a phase that highlights the achievement of a long-held goal. It puts you in contact with others who support this journey towards change. As you make progress, you revamp your vision, creating a trajectory that holds water.

August

Mon 10

Tues 11

Last Quarter Moon in Taurus. 16.45 UTC.

Weds 12

Perseids Meteor Shower. July 17th to August 24th. Peaks night of Aug 12th.

Thurs 13

Venus at Greatest Western Elongation.

August

Fri 14

Sat 15

Sun 16

Message

Gabriel sees a new chapter is arriving soon, this is positive news. You move forward, expanding your horizons towards achieving long-term goals. There is an improvement in your home situation, it hits the sweet spot, and heightens security in your world. A celebration ahead brings a moment that you treasure. This is an ideal time to create space for something new. It does have you evaluating goals and reaching for something significant. Embarking on an inspiring journey sees you developing your higher purpose. Giving back, being of service, holds you in good stead, it is food for your soul.

August

Mon 17

Tues 18

Weds 19
New Moon in Leo. 2:41 UTC

Thurs 20
Islamic New Year

August

Fri 21

Sat 22

Sun 23

Message

Archangel Raziel says that it's true, you are entering a prosperous cycle, as someone who has overcome significant obstacles, this is a breath of fresh air. It does bring substantial changes that drive progress towards larger life goals. It brings the atmosphere of change, shifting your focus forward and creating room to embrace a new chapter of abundance. It leads to a time which is busy and active, a pleasing surprise arrives. An opportunity to support your dreams comes. Exciting developments lead to a time of adventure which inspires your mind.

August

Mon 24

Tues 25
First Quarter Moon in Scorpio. 17.58 UTC

Weds 26

Thurs 27

August

Fri 28

Sat 29

Sun 30

Message

Archangel Raguel says that you shift your focus towards developing a situation that holds promise. It sees growth and change occurring, potential emerges, this hits a sweet spot. It does see you attracting the assistance of one who helps support your goals. It leads to a time of chasing dreams and the sharing of ideas. There is more stability on offer ahead, building towards future growth, does see a situation becoming more connected. However, it is a time of having to wait it out, it will test your patience, being flexible and understanding, broadens the possibilities, it shows plenty of promise is on the horizon.

August/September

Mon 31

Tues 1

Weds 2
Full Moon in Pisces. Full Corn Moon. 5:22 UTC

Thurs 3

September

Fri 4

Sat 5

Sun 6

Message

Archangel Jophiel says that you are ready to embrace a more socially active phase. Opportunities soon arrive, think of this time as having the ability to upgrade your life. It draws new friendships, and there is an emphasis on improving bonds, existing and new. You open a path towards a happy chapter, setting positive intentions, is a powerful way to begin this process. Being open to the abundance which is seeking to inspire your life soon offers you results. It does bring opportunities for self-expression, you find yourself in a more social environment, it connects you with people who have similar interests.

September

Mon 7
Labor Day

Tues 8

Weds 9

Thurs 10
Last Quarter Moon in Gemini. 9.26 UTC

September

Fri 11

Neptune at Opposition.

Sat 12

Sun 13

Message

Uriel says that the improvement of circumstances is a significant theme that is around your life. It clears the decks and sees you heading towards a fresh chapter. You can feel sentimental during this transition phase, memories, emotions, rise up to be processed. However, a big reveal is coming, this gets you excited about the future, and you begin to see long-term plans taking shape. It does have you directing your energy in alignment with an area that inspires. Indeed, a refreshing change is coming, you can bank on seeing your situation evolving to a new level of potential.

September

Mon 14

Tues 15

Weds 16

Thurs 17
New Moon in Virgo. 11:00 UTC

September

Fri 18

Rosh Hashanah (begins at sunset)

Sat 19

Sun 20

Rosh Hashanah (Ends at sunset)

Message

Ariel says this is a time that involves the release of limitations that have held you back, removing the energy which has clung to your spirit, which is instrumental in restoring balance. There is some beautiful alchemy brewing, which leads to a more social chapter. An invitation to an event draws a sense of excitement and celebration. You uncover an option, which is ripe for expansion. It is a time when something arrives out of the blue, this helps you take the leap towards the realization of your dream. Amid this transformation, you begin to see your future taking shape, things manifest in due course.

September

Mon 21

International Day of Peace

Tues 22

Mabon/Fall Equinox. 13:31 UTC

Weds 23

Thurs 24

First Quarter Moon in Capricorn. 1.55 UTC

September

Fri 25

Sat 26

Sun 27

Yom Kippur (begins at sunset)

Message

Archangel Jophiel says that this is the time that brings new information into your life for a reason. It shakes up your life; it begins a chapter that offers room to grow your potential. Reshuffling the decks sweeps away outworn paths; it opens a portal towards a new area, which gives you the place to develop your talents. It is a time which sees significant changes occurring, this catapults you forward. It relates to improving the stability in your life. It is a time of progressing your situation through careful planning and following through with actions that draw more security into your life.

Mon 28

Yom Kippur (Ends at sunset)

Tues 29

Weds 30

Thurs 1

Full Moon in Aries. Harvest Moon. 21:05 UTC
Mercury at Greatest Eastern Elongation.

October

Fri 2

Sukkot (Begins at sunset)

Sat 3

Sun 4

Message

Your Angel guides see opportunities coming to support a more involved personal life. A sign arrives to guide your focus; it considers the progression in an area that inspires your mind. Everything changes quickly, embracing developing the situation does challenge you, it takes you out of your comfort zone, yet it removes doubt, draws clarity, and you enter phase which is lighter, more transparent. The future places emphasis on improving your life, it leads to a section where you can progress your goals as you enter an active phase of creativity and expansion.

October

Mon 5

Tues 6

Weds 7

Draconids Meteor Shower. Oct 6th-10th. Peak night of Oct 7th.

Thurs 8

October

Fri 9

Sukkot (Ends at sunset)

Sat 10

Last Quarter Moon in Cancer. 0.39 UTC

Sun 11

Message

Surprises are earmarked as being part of this phase, Archangel Sandalphone says to expect a message soon, this news is curious, but it does offer the chance to rejuvenate your situation. It heightens the potential possible when you blend your ideas; this takes your aspirations further. It is a journey towards change, you soon get a clearer picture, this draws optimism, drive, and purpose. It does call for swift action, taking a proactive approach, illustrates transformation. Life is engaging, active, and dynamic. It sees you on a path that takes you on new adventures.

October

Mon 12

Columbus Day
Thanksgiving Day (Canada)
Indigenous People's Day

Tues 13

Mercury Retrograde begins.

Weds 14

Thurs 15

October

Fri 16

New Moon in Libra. 19:31 UTC

Sat 17

Sun 18

Message

Archangel Raziel says that you are someone who has a fixed destination in mind, that is half the battle. Making the decision to broaden your horizons does help you focus in the right direction to create tangible results. Contemplating your options lets, you expand your perception; it signifies there are many possible routes to create the outcome desired. There is an increase of opportunity coming, it has you diving into an empowering chapter, clearing the way to embrace change.

October

Mon 19

Tues 20

Weds 21

Orionids Meteor Shower. Oct 2nd - Nov 7th. Peaks night of Nov 21st.

Thurs 22

Fri 23

First Quarter Moon in Capricorn. 13.23 UTC

Sat 24

Sun 25

Message

Archangel Raguel says that you enter a stable phase that focuses on creating positive change. An opportunity arrives, it sees you moving out of your usual routine, and abundant chapter is ready to blossom. This is a transition forward, motivated, and inspired, you pursue leads, revealing a path towards growth. Life heads towards an upswing, this is in alignment with your higher goals. As your horizons expand, your imagination is leading the way forward. It is a time of excitement, inspiration, and creativity, it does have you dreaming big about future goals

October

Mon 26

Tues 27

Weds 28

Thurs 29

October/November

Fri 30

Sat 31

Full Moon, Blue Moon in Taurus. Hunters Moon. 14:49 UTC
Uranus at Opposition.
Samhain/Halloween.

Sun 1

All Saints' Day

Message

Jophiel says that spending time with friends helps put the focus on developing bonds. It does see bigger doors open, as you embrace connecting with someone who inspires your mind. It's a time which is a lively and active, this keeps you on your feet. Things are set to shift forward, a fresh cycle beckons to you which offers you room to embark on a journey towards the achievement of your goals. News arrives, which points the way forward. It moves you towards a dynamic situation, you have a companion who enters your life, this person restores balance, it is a time which reconnects you to your personal vision.

November

Mon 2

Tues 3

Mercury Retrograde ends.

Weds 4

Taurids Meteor Shower. Sept 7th - Dec 10th. Peaks on Nov 4th.

Thurs 5

November

Fri 6

Sat 7

Sun 8

Last Quarter Moon in Leo. 13.46 UTC

Message

Archangel Uriel is pleased to share that you soon reach a turning point, which marks the beginning of a glorious chapter of growth. It is a time that sees new options arriving; this gives you a new lead to investigate. It's well worth your investment of time, you find that things come together with a flourish. Being assertive, releasing that which has been holding you back, helps you lift the barriers and bravely embark on a new path of achieving a larger goal. It is a time that inspires your mind and draws innovative ideas. An exciting prospect arrives, which gives you the chance to revamp your life.

November

Mon 9

Tues 10

Weds 11

Remembrance Day (Canada)
Veterans Day

Thurs 12

November

Fri 13

Sat 14

Sun 15

New Moon in Scorpio. 5:07 UTC

Message

Archangel Zadkiel says that while there are hurdles to navigate, staying true to your spirit does guide you intuitively to the right course of action. A proactive phase has you taking the initiative and digging deep to get a resolution to a sensitive area. You soon are to make a connection with someone who influences your decision-making process, it leads to inspiring conversations, and does set the stage for future progress. This process of healing the past is highly beneficial, you embark on a journey of discovery. It lights a path towards new options, setting the stage for fantastic growth.

November

Mon 16

Tues 17

Leonids Meteor Shower. Nov 6th-30th. Peaks night of Nov 17th.

Weds 18

Thurs 19

November

Fri 20

Sat 21

Sun 22

First Quarter Moon in Pisces. 4.45 UTC

Message

Archangel Haniel says that you soon put your best foot forward and transform your life into magic. It leads to a path that is in alignment with your higher purpose. There is radiant and fanciful creative energy coming, creatively inspired, you find your thoughts shimmer like crystal that dances in the light. This heightened awareness of innovative energy results in emotions that are bewitching and radiant. It results in shimmering feelings of enchantment. You hone your skills of storytelling in a social environment. Your vivid imagination effortlessly brings splendid thoughts to life.

November

Mon 23

Tues 24

Weds 25

Thurs 26
Thanksgiving Day (US)

November

Fri 27

Sat 28

Sun 29

Message

Archangel Uriel speaks of some curious changes arriving, which are instrumental at sweeping away areas that no longer serve your needs, this heads towards a shift that is much more suited to your future goals. It is a great time to make room for something new, news arrives at an event which offers you a place to mingle. Incredible changes are coming in your home and personal life, which can open doors to a brighter future.

Mon 30

Full Moon in Gemini. Beaver Moon. 9:30 UTC
Penumbral Lunar Eclipse.

Tues 1

Weds 2

Thurs 3

December

Fri 4

Sat 5

Sun 6

Message

Chamuel says that you turn a corner, heading towards growth. Your willingness
to persevere and be patient with the process leads to tangible results. The
intentions you have set are instrumental in paving the way forward. It does
bring more security to your life. The seeds planted, can blossom. An invitation
arrives at the end of a monthly event. It does have you thinking about the
potential possible, you shift your focus forwards, a newfound sense of freedom
draws exciting potential into your life. Reawakening to the abundance in your
world, you take some bold moves towards achieving your goals.

December

Mon 7

Tues 8

Last Quarter Moon in Virgo. 0.37 UTC

Weds 9

Thurs 10

Hanukkah (begins at sunset)

December

Fri 11

Sat 12

Sun 13

Geminids Meteor Shower. Dec 7th-17th. Peaks nights of Dec 13th-15th.

Message

Archangel Haniel says that this is the time that may see planning coming to the forefront of your life. An offer crosses your path, it gets you an option, you can expand. Doing your homework does enable due diligence to light a way towards success. It is a time where you take the plunge, as transformation lights, a compelling way forward, this is something you can grow into the New Year and beyond. Mapping out a solid plan is a component of the success ahead. Focusing on the tangible steps, you move forward and reveal the right lead to chase.

December

Mon 14
New Moon in Sagittarius. 16:17 UTC

Tues 15

Weds 16

Thurs 17

December

Fri 18

Hanukkah (Ends at sunset)

Sat 19

Sun 20

Message

A rare opportunity may cross your path this week, says Archangel Sandalphone. An impromptu gathering creates a sense of excitement in your world soon. It does rev up a season of get-togethers and invitations to mingle. It emphasizes a phase of personal growth and harmony, which offers you the opportunity to rebalance your energy after an unsettling time. Putting your creative ideas out there is also favorable, it does connect you with a broader audience of kindred spirits.

December

Mon 21

Ursids Meteor Shower. Dec 17th – 25th. Peaks night of Dec 21st.
Great Conjunction of Jupiter and Saturn.
Yule/ Winter Solstice. 10:02 UTC
First Quarter Moon in Pisces. 23.41 UTC

Tues 22

Weds 23

Thurs 24

December

Fri 25

Christmas Day

Sat 26

Boxing Day (Canada & UK)
Kwanzaa begins

Sun 27

Message

A key event stands out as being prominent this week, says Archangel Zadkiel. It is a chapter that expands the boundaries of your life. You can draw in fresh inspiration, and this is healing and cathartic to your soul. Outworn areas are no longer problematic, you are willing to look ahead and embrace the development of substantial goals. Life picks up the pace, and you can trust your instincts to reliably guide you forward. Honoring that voice within, you receive information subliminally, which points to the correct area for progression.

December

Mon 28

Tues 29

Weds 30

Full Moon in Cancer. Cold Moon. 3:28 UTC

Thurs 31

New Year's Eve

January

Fri 1

New Year's Day
Kwanzaa ends

Sat 2

Sun 3

Message

Your Angels support you with love and blessings, they say that this is a valuable time that expands the boundaries of your life. You are ready to pull the trigger and unleash a new chapter into your world. You are someone who can harness a positive outlook and utilize your inherent sense of optimism to lead towards a new avenue, ready to be explored. It is a time of magic possibilities, as a new cycle of change is unfolding. Your thoughts are manifesting goals, which, in turn, become a progression of actions that you undertake to achieve the desired results.

About Crystal Sky

Crystal is passionate about the universe, helping others, and personal development. She writes yearly horoscopes books for each individual star sign and also produces a range of astrologically minded diaries to celebrate the universal forces which affect us all. You can visit learn more about Crystals books and personal readings by visiting her website. www.mystic-shores.com

When not writing about the stars, you can find Crystal under them, gazing up at the abundance that surrounds us all, with her pooch Henri by her side.